W9-AWD-310

NOT FOR RESAL
This is a Free Book
Bookthing.org

Great Scientific
Questions and the
Scientists Who
Answered Them

HOW DO WE KNOW

THE LAWS OF
THERMODYNAMICS

JEFFREY B. MORAN

Great Scientific
Questions and the
Scientists Who
Answered Them

HOW DO WE KNOW

THE LAWS OF
THERMODYNAMICS

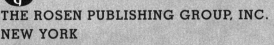

THE ROSEN PUBLISHING GROUP, INC.
NEW YORK

Published in 2001 by The Rosen Publishing Group, Inc.
29 East 21st Street, New York, NY 10010

Copyright © 2001 by Jeffrey B. Moran

First Edition

All rights reserved. No part of this book may be reproduced in any form without permission in writing from the publisher, except by a reviewer.

Library of Congress Cataloging-in-Publication Data

Moran, Jeffrey B.
How do we know the laws of thermodynamics / by Jeffrey B. Moran.—1st ed.
p. cm. — (Great scientific questions and the scientists who answered them)
Includes bibliographical references and index.
ISBN 0-8239-3384-9 (lib. bdg.)
1. Heat—Juvenile literature. 2. Temperature measurement—Juvenile literature. 3. Thermodynamics—Juvenile literature.
[1. Heat. 2. Thermodynamics.] I. Title. II. Series.
QC256.M56 2001

2001000002

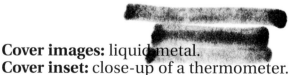

Cover images: liquid metal.
Cover inset: close-up of a thermometer.

Manufactured in the United States of America

Contents

Introduction

Boiling water is hot. Ice is cold. The contrast between hot and cold is detected naturally by sense receptors in our skin that give us the ability to sense heat and its opposite. We measure heat with a thermometer and we assign it a temperature. But what exactly is heat? What is

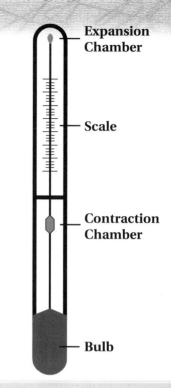

Expansion Chamber

Scale

Contraction Chamber

Bulb

temperature? What makes things hot or cold? How does temperature change? Why should we care if things are hot or cold? Why should we try to understand how heat moves from one place to another?

Dictionary definitions of "hot" and "cold" relate those sensations to our normal body temperature. Warm things have temperatures above

The thermometer works because certain substances expand at a uniform rate when heated.

our body temperature and cold things have temperatures below our body temperature. In this way humans are able to compare how things feel temperature-wise to themselves to get a subjective sense of hotness or coldness. In one sense, heat is a sensation in the mind. But we know that some physical process is causing our nerves to be stimulated in this way. That is what we really mean

When heated sufficiently, water's state changes from liquid to gas.

when we ask what heat is, and what is happening in nature that causes us to feel sensations of hot and cold.

It isn't only human beings who respond to heat flow and changes in temperature. Heat affects all material objects at the molecular and atomic level. Temperature determines whether most substances exist in a solid, liquid, or gaseous state, and changing the temperature enough can change the state of matter. At extremely high temperatures, matter can be transformed into plasma, a fourth state of matter made up of ionized atoms. So basic is the phenomenon of temperature that physicists consider it a fundamental property of matter, along with volume, mass, electric charge, and time.

The word "thermodynamics" consists of *thermo*, meaning heat, and *dynamics*, which refers to movement. In its broadest sense, thermodynamics is about heat and how heat moves. That heat moves at all was itself a discovery of considerable importance. It is not at all obvious. You light a campfire and it warms you. It has heat. The fire goes out, and the heat disappears. Common experience will not tell you that none of that heat has really disappeared. Heat is a form of energy, and energy can be neither created nor destroyed. That, as you will learn, is one of the most important of the laws of thermodynamics. The heat from the fire has not disappeared. It has been carried off and transformed into other forms of energy. So we are going to have to explore what energy is.

That is what thermodynamics is really all about, not so much heat in particular as the study of energy and how it behaves. We may think of energy as the "lift" we get when we consume a sugar-rich drink, but physicists have a very precise definition of energy. Energy is the ability to do work, and work is the application of a force to move a mass through a certain distance. Now we can begin to understand why it is so important to study heat flow and temperature. We generate heat in order to do work. The classic example of this is the steam engine, in which heat energy is used to boil water, creating steam to push a piston attached to a rotary shaft. The shaft can then be used to turn a train's wheels or a ship's propeller or the machines in a factory. In this process, heat energy is converted into mechanical energy. Understanding what heat and temperature are and how energy is transformed into different forms is essential to understanding the modern industrial world and how we get things done. As we shall see, much of our theoretical understanding of thermodynamics did not come about until people could examine the functioning of real machines like the steam engine.

We have already disclosed that heat is a form of energy. Let's anticipate our scientific history a bit and define heat and temperature right here. There have been many misconceptions and erroneous theories about heat, and understanding why these ideas were wrong will be easier if we at least hint at the correct answers before we begin. If heat is a form of energy, energy is the ability to do work, and work is the movement of a mass through a distance, then heat must have something to do with the movement of material objects. Heat, in fact, is the energy of molecular motion. All matter is made up of atoms bound into molecules, and all molecules are in continuous motion. In a liquid or a gas, those molecules move about freely. In a solid, the molecules are not so free to move around, but they still vibrate within a crystal-like structure. This is heat energy. Add heat to a substance and its molecules move or vibrate, more rapidly. Put a thermometer into a substance and you can measure the average motion of the molecules striking the instrument. That is temperature. When you touch a hot object, the nerves in your fingers respond to the rapid motion of the molecules in that object, causing a sensation of warmth.

INTRODUCTION

Heat and temperature are distinct concepts. The ocean may be colder, that is, have a lower temperature, than a glass of heated water, but the ocean contains a much greater quantity of heat energy. So it's important to remember that temperature measures the average energy of molecules, not the total amount of heat in a substance. This, as we shall see, creates some phenomena that might at first seem to defy common sense. Heat always flows from a region of high temperature to a region of low temperature, regardless of the total amount of heat present in each region. That little glass of heated water, if poured into the ocean, would transfer heat energy to the ocean, and the ocean's temperature would rise a small amount, even though the ocean contained much more heat energy than did the glass of water. But there is no way in which you can transfer any of the heat energy in the ocean back into the heated water in the glass, because the ocean has a lower temperature than the water in the glass.

We'll approach this subject in two parts, beginning first with the history of efforts to define and measure temperature. Out of that effort will emerge a second and more theoretical effort to understand the nature of the "substance" called heat and to derive the general scientific laws describing the behavior of this type of energy. When you understand the laws of thermodynamics, you are powerfully armed against sloppy or fraudulent scientific thinking. You are not going to be fooled by those who claim to have invented perpetual motion machines or who claim they can run your car forever on a pint of water or who claim that nuclear fusion can occur in a glass of cold water. You will understand why these assertions can't be true, and you will understand a great deal more as well. You may even understand something about the fate of the universe.

Early Ideas About Heat and Temperature

We'll start in ancient Greece, where a philosopher named Anaximander (610–546 BC), a pupil of the great Thales of Miletus (624–546 BC), considered the founder of Greek science, recognized a fact that dominated all subsequent Greek theories of nature. The world presents us with a series of contrasts and opposites. Anaximander believed that the most fundamental of these oppositions were the ones associated with moisture (wet versus dry) and temperature (hot versus cold). Mixtures of these opposites, and others, determined the qualities of various substances.

Another Greek philosopher, Empedocles (495–435 BC), elaborated on this theory of opposites and developed a theory of the nature of matter that described the world as composed of four basic elements: water, air, earth, and fire. Fire was considered the substance that made up the heavens and was the rarest and most powerful of the elements. And since living bodies were usually warmer than inanimate objects, fire was in some way a fundamental quality of living things—the spark of life. Although Empedocles was developing a theory of matter rather than a theory of heat, he recognized that things had different temperatures and that temperature was an important property of nature.

EARLY IDEAS ABOUT HEAT AND TEMPERATURE

The Greek philosopher Aristotle (384–322 BC) adopted Empedocles's theory of matter. Aristotle taught a wide range of scientific, philosophical, and political topics, and the school he founded in Athens, the Lyceum, provided the premier education of the time. So convincing were Aristotle's logical arguments that his views on scientific matters dominated European thinking for more than a thousand years. In fact, during that long period, learning became a matter of reciting the "authorities," particularly Aristotle. Thus his teachings, including the ideas of a geocentric, or Earth-centered, universe and the four primary elements of Empedocles became unquestioned facts that no scholar seriously challenged until the early seventeenth century.

Though they did not understand the true nature of heat, the ancient Greeks learned to use it to operate simple mechanical devices. Little is known of the life of Hero of Alexandria, who was thought to have been born around 20 BC. By this time the Romans had conquered Egypt, and the great age of Greek philosophy was coming to an end. Hero was one of the period's last great Greek experimenters. He wrote treatises on working with simple machines like the lever, the pulley, the wedge, the wheel, the gear, and the screw. He also wrote a manuscript called *Pneumatics* that described a number of steam-powered mechanical devices. These included fountains in which the pressure of steam forced columns of water upward through tubes and a device that opened and closed temple doors. In the latter device, heat from an altar fire caused air in a vessel half-filled with water to expand. This forced the water through a hose into another vessel attached to a system of pulleys and counterweights.

Hero also described a primitive steam engine called an aeolipile. It consisted of a reservoir of boiling water connected by a tube to a large hollow sphere with open, bent tubes coming out of it. The sphere was attached to a gimbal so that it could rotate. Heated steam entering the hollow sphere caused it to spin as it blew the steam out of the bent tubes. The aeolipile was

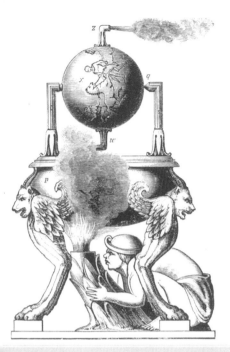

Hero's aeolipile

the first known device to transform heat into rotary motion, in effect the first steam turbine.

The devices that Hero described served only as toys or novelties and had no practical function. The aeolipile could be used to rotate a small platform of dancing figurines, for example. The thought does not seem to have occurred to anyone in ancient Greece that such devices might be used to substitute mechanical power for human muscles. That is because these ancient societies were based on cheap slave labor, and Greek intellectuals had no reason or inclination to figure out how to do things with less effort. All the same, these devices illustrate that people 2,000 years ago recognized that heat energy could be used to do work. Neither Hero nor his contemporaries, however, describe any experiments performed on heat or steam, and they had no instruments for measuring or quantifying temperature.

The Greek physician Galen (AD 130–AD 200), who established many of the accepted rules for medical practice for the next 1,500 years, made one of the first attempts to create a standard temperature scale. Galen served as a physician to gladiators, and he knew that many diseases and infections caused by injuries made people feel warmer than normal. He proposed a standard "neutral" temperature arrived at by combining equal amounts of boiling water and ice. On either side of this neutral temperature, Galen proposed four degrees of cold and four degrees of heat, with the temperature of ice being the coldest possible and the temperature of boiling water being the hottest possible. Although he proposed eight degrees of temperature, Galen did not have a temperature-measuring device with which to distinguish those degrees. His efforts at quantifying temperature consisted primarily of putting his hand on a patient's forehead and estimating whether the patient felt warmer or colder than normal.

After Galen, no one advanced the methods of temperature measurement for almost 1,500 years. Consequently, there was little increase in our understanding of the nature of heat. Without accurate, reliable thermometers to measure and record temperatures, it was virtually impossible to conduct appropriate experiments. In these intervening centuries, research into the nature of heat was extensive but unsystematic. It was discovered that a pane of glass blocked the heat of a fire, but not the light of the Sun; that the darker an object, the faster it would warm up in sunlight; and that heat can pass through a vacuum but sound cannot. But there was no scientific understanding of what heat was or why it behaved the way it did.

THE FIRST THERMOMETERS

In the late sixteenth century, the need for an accurate scale of temperature became increasingly obvious not only to scientists but to physicians. In 1578, Johannes Hasler published a book entitled *De Logistica Medica* (*About Medicine*), which dealt with the problem of finding the "natural degree of temperature of each man, as determined by his age, the time of year, the elevation of the pole (latitude), and other influences." Hasler believed that the body temperature of people living in the Tropics was higher than the body temperature of people living in temperate regions, and he devised a complicated chart comparing Galen's eight temperature degrees to latitude. Doctors used this chart as a guide when mixing medicines, though they still had no real idea about how to measure temperature.

Around 1600, two Italian scientists, Galileo Galilei (1564–1642) and Santorio Santorio (1561–1636), became interested in quantifying the measurement of heat. To measure heat, you need some substance or object that reacts in a consistent and measurable way to changes in temperature. This is known as the thermometric medium. From Hero's book *Pneumatics*, which was rediscovered and first published in Europe in 1575, as well as from their own experiences, both men knew that heat caused air to expand. Air, therefore, seemed an obvious choice as a substance that could be used to measure temperature.

Galileo, the most famous scientist of his time, was born in Pisa, Italy, where he showed an aptitude for mathematics and mechanics at an early age. After studying at the University of Pisa, he became a lecturer there, and later became a professor of mathematics at the Universities of Padua and Florence. He made many contributions to the development of science, such as improvements to the design of telescopes and experiments on motion and acceleration. Some of this work led him to reject the prevailing wisdom that Earth was at the center of the universe, and he became an early advocate of the Copernican system, which placed the Sun at the center of the solar system, and which placed Galileo in hot water with the Catholic Church.

Among his many other accomplishments, Galileo made a device called a thermoscope that responded to changes in temperature. In a letter written in 1638, one of his former students, Benedetto Castelli, wrote: "I recall an experiment shown to me thirty-five years ago by our master Galileo, who taking a glass flask the size of a small hen's egg with a neck around two palms in length and as thin as a barley-stalk, heated the flask with the palms of his hands and then, turning the mouth of it over into a vessel placed under it, in which there was a little water, when he left the vessel free of the heat of his hands, suddenly the water began to climb up the neck and rose to above the level of the water in the vase by more than a palm."

Galileo's thermoscope consisted of a relatively large, round, glass bulb at the top of a long, thin, glass tube. The open, bottom end of the tube was placed in a

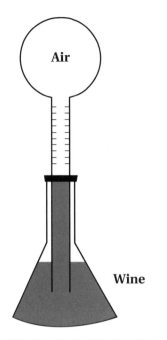

Air

Wine

Galileo's thermoscope

vessel containing wine. When the air in the bulb cooled, that air contracted and the reduction in volume allowed fluid to rise up into the tube. When the air in the bulb was heated, it expanded and forced the wine in the tube downward. Note that the diameter of the tube was small compared to the volume of the air-filled, glass bulb. Thus, a relatively small change in the temperature of the air in the bulb could produce dramatic change in the level of the wine in the tube of the thermoscope. This device worked in reverse from what we are accustomed to in thermometers today. A colder temperature raised the level of wine in the tube, and a warmer temperature lowered the wine level.

Santorio Santorio, after serving as a physician to a Croatian nobleman, began a medical practice in Venice in 1599 and became a friend of Galileo. In 1611, he took a position as professor of medicine at the University of Padua, where he had originally obtained his medical degree. Santorio performed experiments to study human metabolism. He placed himself on a platform suspended from the arm of an enormous balance and weighed precisely all of his solid and liquid intake and excretions. He concluded that by far the greatest part of the food he ate and drank was lost from the body via *perspiratio insensibilis*, or "insensible perspiration." Although some water loss occurs through perspiration, we recognize now that most of what we consume that is not excreted is lost as heat. But these experiments inspired many subsequent experiments on metabolism.

Santorio argued that the fundamental properties of nature were mathematical—things such as number, position, size, and form. His passion for describing natural phenomena numerically, led him to invent several measuring instruments, including a wind gauge, a water-current meter, and a pulsilogium, a device that used a pendulum to measure pulse rate. He also produced a thermoscope at about the same time that Galileo made his. It was his idea to put the bulb of the thermoscope inside a patient's mouth to measure the patient's temperature. This was the first time that a thermometer was used in a medical setting. Santorio is also considered the first to add a numerical scale to a thermoscope. This was the beginning of attempts to assign real numbers to degrees of heat.

The thermoscopes of Galileo and Santorio are considered "air thermometers" because air was the substance affected by temperature changes. A change in the intensity of heat was translated into a volume change in the air. These instruments were very crude, however. The air in them also responded to changes in pressure, so that the thermometers also worked as barometers, which made it very difficult to obtain accurate and consistent measurements. The thermometer was not yet either a practical medical tool or a useful scientific instrument.

Among the last to experiment with air thermometers, and to try to turn them into practical devices, was Cornelius Jacobszoon Drebbel (1572–1633). Drebbel had little formal education and was more of an inventor and mechanic than a scientist. He was born in the Netherlands but moved to England in 1604 when the English king, James I, became intrigued with some of his gadgets. Drebbel devised a thermoscope in which expanding or contracting air pushed a column of mercury in a tube, opening or closing a damper that regulated the amount of air going to a fire. If the fire burned too hot, the expanding air column would close off the fire's air supply and would reduce the rate of heat generation. Drebbel had invented the first thermostat, or temperature regulator. He modified the device for various types of furnaces and ovens, and even for an egg incubator. Unfortunately, in spite of work he did for the Royal Navy on the construction of a submarine, Drebbel was regarded more as a tinkerer than a man of learning, and when King James I died, Drebbel's place in the funeral procession was with the court jesters.

Temperature Measurement

n the quarter century following their invention, thermoscopes appeared in many places in Europe. However, it soon became apparent that atmospheric pressure as well as temperature affected the volume of air in these devices. Most of these early thermoscopes worked just as effectively as did barometers, but changes in atmospheric pressure made temperature readings unreliable. Those who were interested in the accurate measurement of temperature began searching for an alternative to air as a thermometric medium.

The open-ended tubes of air thermometers were frequently placed in dishes of wine rather than water. Wine did not freeze at temperatures that caused ice to form, nor did it boil at temperatures that caused water to boil. It was also known that the volume of wine increased when warmed, like air. Thus wine, or "spirits" as alcoholic substances are sometimes called, seemed to be a logical choice for an alternative to air in thermometers.

Around 1654, Ferdinand II, the grand duke of Tuscany (1610–1670), developed just such a spirit thermometer. Tuscany, a region of central Italy north of Rome with Florence as its capital, was one of the places where the Italian Renaissance flourished. Ferdinand, a member of the Medici family, was a poor ruler but excelled as a scientist and a patron of other scientists.

He was a supporter of Galileo but is sometimes blamed for not opposing the Catholic Church's attack on Galileo. The thermometer he developed had the same general design as did the air thermometer—a round bulb with a long, thin tube coming out of it. But Ferdinand turned it upside down so that the bulb was at the bottom and the tube extended upward, and, after filling the bulb with wine, he sealed the end of the tube. With a sealed tube, the instrument would no longer be affected by changes in atmospheric pressure. Ferdinand then etched the tube with fifty equally spaced marks so that degrees of temperature could be measured. Ferdinand's thermometer scale had no zero point, however. Without a standard reference point, it was difficult to compare degrees recorded with Ferdinand's thermometers to degrees recorded with other instruments. Nonetheless, spirit thermometers began to replace air thermometers.

To turn a temperature-sensitive device into a real thermometer, one needs selected, fixed points on the scale that correspond to common phenomena that are reproducible and that always occur at the same temperature. Ferdinand's spirit thermometers reached England in 1661, where members of the Royal Society soon saw the importance of standardizing thermometer measurements. Robert Hooke (1635–1703), curator of the Royal Society, constructed a spirit thermometer. Rather than begin by making regular marks on the stem as Ferdinand had, he first put the bulb of the thermometer into ice water, which he thought would be a good fixed temperature point. He made a zero mark on the thermometer next to the level of the liquid in the tube. He then made other marks on the glass tube, each of which represented an expansion of 1/500th of the volume of the liquid in the bulb. Hooke made many other thermometers and showed that any thermometer, regardless of size or shape, using the same thermometric medium (red wine), could be standardized in this manner. Hooke's original thermometer was used to collect the first useful meteorological records. Instead of wine, Hooke had used alcohol with a red dye.

After Hooke introduced the idea of fixed temperature points, Isaac Newton (1642–1727) and others experimented with a long list of what they considered useful fixed points. Using a thermometer filled with linseed or olive oil, Newton put the bulb into numerous substances. The temperatures of molten metals were too high to be of much use. Putting a thermometer into the embers of a small fire produced an erratic reading. But the boiling point of water, like the freezing point of water, was a reliable measure.

Danish astronomer Ole Roemer (1644–1710), who discovered the finite speed of light, made an important contribution to the science of thermometry. When Roemer was working at the old observatory of astronomer Tycho Brahe, he found that changes in air

Ole Roemer is pictured here in his laboratory. Roemer devised a more accurate thermometer using the freezing and boiling points of water.

temperature affected his astronomical instruments. As early as 1692, he used a thermometer to measure temperature so he could compensate for its effects. Around 1702, Roemer began producing spirit thermometers of his own design. He had the insight to use two fixed points for calibrating his thermometers rather than using a single point. Roemer chose the temperature of crushed ice as one fixed point and the temperature of boiling water as the other. He divided the tube of the thermometer between these two points into sixty degrees. Using two standard reference points made thermometers more accurate. But Roemer never published the details of his work.

FAHRENHEIT AND CELSIUS

By the beginning of the eighteenth century, scientists had recognized that temperature had profound effects on the volume and pressure of gases and liquids. Some scientists were beginning to study the behavior of gases because they believed that the behavior of a gas revealed much about the nature of matter. At the time, the "kinetic theory of matter," the theory that matter was made up of tiny particles and that heat and pressure were caused by the behavior of those particles, was yet to be proved. To conduct the proper experiments, the accurate measurement of temperature became important.

By the early 1700s, however, at least twenty different temperature scales were in use, most of them based on a single reference point. Sometimes, a thermometer was simply attached to a board with several temperature scales on pieces of paper glued next to it, so that someone reading the thermometer could use any of the several scales. Only two of these temperature scales remain common today: the temperature scales of Fahrenheit and Celsius.

Daniel Fahrenheit (1686–1736) was a German maker of meteorological instruments who spent most of his adult life in Holland. Although Roemer never published the details of his thermometer designs, Fahrenheit heard about them, and in 1708 he traveled to Copenhagen to meet the Danish astronomer and study his thermometers. After working with Roemer for several months, Fahrenheit returned to Holland and began to improve on Roemer's designs.

Fahrenheit also made barometers that used a column of mercury to measure air pressure. He knew that changing temperatures caused small changes in the height of a column of mercury inside a barometer, and he concluded that a thin mercury column might make a good temperature-sensitive system. Fahrenheit built a mercury thermometer in 1714. In experimental work, he showed that because the freezing and boiling points of mercury were lower and higher respectively than those of alcohol, temperature measurements could extend well beyond the freezing and boiling points of water. Mercury also expanded and contracted more uniformly than wine, so temperatures could be measured more accurately. Fahrenheit

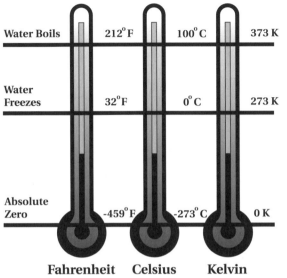

Water Boils	212°F	100°C	373 K
Water Freezes	32°F	0°C	273 K
Absolute Zero	-459°F	-273°C	0 K
	Fahrenheit	Celsius	Kelvin

These thermometers show the relationship between Fahrenheit, Celsius, and Kelvin temperature scales.

used the same zero reference point as Roemer had used by measuring the temperature of a mixture of ice and salt water.

Because Roemer was designing instruments for meteorological use, however, he felt that the temperature of the boiling point of water was too high for a second reference point. Instead he used human body temperature. He also wanted a very accurate scale with fine gradations, so he marked the tube of his mercury thermometer with 96 units, or "degrees." Later on, he made some minor adjustments to his scale so that he had exactly 180° between the freezing and boiling points of water. On Fahrenheit's temperature scale, water froze at 32° and boiled at 212°. Human body temperature, one of his original reference points, was adjusted to 98.6° on the revised scale.

Fahrenheit's thermometer was the most accurate temperature-measuring device of the time. Because of its improved accuracy, the Fahrenheit temperature scale soon became widely accepted in the Netherlands and England. It is still in use in the United States. Fahrenheit used his thermometers to show that many liquids had characteristic boiling points under standard conditions and that boiling points change with changes in atmospheric pressure.

A generation later, in 1742, Anders Celsius (1701–1744), a professor of astronomy in Uppsala, Sweden, developed a new temperature scale that is still used for scientific work in most parts of the world. The idea was suggested to him by one of his academic colleagues, the botanist Carolus Linnaeus (1707–1778). Celsius divided the temperature scale between the freezing and boiling points of water into an even 100°. At first he placed the freezing point of water at 100° and the boiling point of water at 0°, working in reverse from his predecessors. But the following year he reversed himself and set the freezing point of water at 0° and the boiling point of water at 100°. This is sometimes called the centigrade scale. In 1948, however, the Ninth General Conference of Weights and Measures officially decreed that what had been "degrees centigrade" should henceforth be called degrees Celsius. The Celsius scale, based on a number that was a multiple of ten, became part of the general metric system of measurements used by scientists throughout the world. It was used to define other scientific units. For example, the calorie, a metric unit of heat, is defined as the amount of heat required to raise the temperature of one gram or one cubic centimeter of water one degree Celsius.

Other temperature scales and methods of measuring temperature have been devised. In 1780,

The Fahrenheit scale sets the freezing point of water at 32° above zero and the boiling point of water at 212°, for a difference of 180° between the two reference points. The Celsius scales sets the freezing point of water at 0° and the boiling point of water at 100°, for a difference of 100° between the two reference points. Therefore 100° on the Celsius scale is equivalent to 180° on the Fahrenheit scale, or one degree Celsius is equal to 9/5 of a Fahrenheit degree. But the two scales begin at different points, so the full formula for converting between the two scales is as follows:

Degrees Celsius = (Degrees Fahrenheit – 32) x 5/9

Degrees Fahrenheit = (Degrees Celsius x 9/5) + 32

A degree on the Kelvin scale is equal to a degree on the Celsius scale, but the zero point on the Kelvin scale is set at absolute zero, where all molecular motion stops, and this happens to be at –273.15° on the Celsius scale. So to determine the temperature in kelvins, just add 273.15° to the Celsius reading.

TEMPERATURE MEASUREMENT

French physician Jacques Charles (1746–1823) discovered that, if pressure is held constant, all gases expanded at the same rate as the temperature was raised. He was a good candidate for this discovery, because his passion was hot air ballooning. Charles discovered that for each degree Celsius that he raised the temperature of a volume of gas, it would expand by 1/273 of its volume at 0°. Working backward, this meant that if he lowered the temperature of the gas, at 273° below zero it would have zero volume. That meant that minus 273° on the Celsius scale was the lowest possible temperature. This idea was taken up a half century later by the English physicist William Thomson, also known as Baron Kelvin, who introduced a new temperature scale that defined this lowest possible temperature as "absolute zero," with the boiling point of water set at 373°. On this scale, degrees are known as kelvins.

Charles never published his findings on expanding gases. The experiments were repeated by French chemist Joseph-Louis Gay-Lussac (1778–1850), who did publish his work. What might have been called Charles's Law is now known as Gay-Lussac's Law. Knowing the relationship between the volume, temperature, and pressure of a gas made it possible to build thermometers based on the expansion of gases.

Jacques Charles first discovered Guy-Lussac's law.

In 1821, German physicist Thomas Seebeck (1770–1831) fused together two wires of different metals and measured the electrical voltage generated when the wires were heated. This "thermocouple" proved a reliable way of measuring temperature. In the 1870s, German inventor William Siemens (1823–1883), who was living in England, invented a thermometer

TEMPERATURE MEASUREMENT

based on measuring the changes in electrical resistance inside a bar of platinum as it was heated. By the middle of the nineteenth century, there were a number of different methods of accurately measuring temperature, most of them using the degree scales of either Fahrenheit or Celsius. At that time, scientists were in a better position to examine just what it was that temperature measured. What was heat?

The Nature of Heat

t was British chemist Joseph Black (1728–1799) who was the first to distinguish between heat and temperature. He saw that the total quantity of heat within a body was not the same thing as the intensity of that heat. Temperature measured the intensity of heat, not the total quantity of heat. He drew this distinction in 1764 when he studied the changes in the state of water. Black observed that when a block of ice was heated, it melted, but its temperature did not increase until all the ice had been transformed into water. The same thing happened when water turned into steam. To make these changes of state, water would absorb quantities of heat, but they would not be reflected in a temperature increase.

Black had put equal amounts of water in two identical globular glass containers. He froze the water in one bulb and brought the water in the other bulb to a temperature just above the freezing point, and then suspended the two bulbs by wires in a large, empty room that had a temperature of 8° Celsius. He recorded the temperature of the water in the bulbs every few minutes. In thirty minutes, the temperature of the liquid water was 5°, but the temperature of the ice remained at 0°. It took ten and one-half hours for all of the ice to melt and the liquid in that bulb to reach 5°. Black concluded that it took twenty-one times as much heat to melt the ice as it did to raise the temperature of liquid water. Black called the heat absorbed by a substance while changing state but not increasing in temperature "latent heat."

British chemist Joseph Black

Black also recognized that at cold temperatures, a block of iron felt colder than did an equal-sized block of wood at the same temperature, and at hot temperatures, a block of iron felt hotter than did a block of wood at the same temperature. Black concluded that iron had a greater capacity than wood to conduct heat. This led him to develop the concept of "specific heat." Specific heat is the amount of heat required to raise the temperature of one gram of a substance 1° Celsius. Different substances have different specific heats. In general, metals have low specific heats. They get hot quickly. Wood and other nonmetallic materials have high specific heats and must absorb a lot of heat before their temperatures increase.

CALORIC VERSUS KINETIC

Together, the concepts of latent heat and specific heat helped to make a clear distinction between temperature and quantity of heat. Black himself, however, had difficulty accepting the results of his experiments. At the time, there were two theories of what heat was, and Black supported the wrong one. The older theory, in which Black believed, went all the way back to Aristotle and claimed that heat was a weightless, insensible fluid, called caloric, that flowed from hot substances to cold substances. But some thinkers, men like René Descartes, Robert Boyle, and Christian Huygens, believed that heat was caused by

With different substances, it takes a different quantity of heat energy to bring about an equal rise in temperature. Specific heat is a ratio, that is, the amount of heat needed to raise the temperature of one gram of a substance 1° Celsius *compared to* the amount of heat needed to raise the temperature of one gram of water 1° Celsius. The specific heat of iron, for example, is .11. It requires only about one-tenth as much heat to raise the temperature of a gram of iron 1° Celsius as it does a gram of water.

the motion of invisible particles. Even Isaac Newton thought that heat was caused by "the motion of small parts of bodies." This was known as the kinetic theory of matter, as kinetic energy was the energy of motion. But this kinetic theory depended on the existence of atoms and molecules, which, in the seventeenth and eighteenth centuries, could not be proven to exist.

In 1798, Benjamin Thompson (1753–1814), also known as Count Rumford, observed that favored the kinetic theory of matter. Thompson was an American who, during the Revolutionary War, was a Tory who had allegiance to the English king. When the British abandoned Boston, Massachusetts, Thompson left for England. There he was accused of being a spy for France, so he left for Bavaria, where the local prince made him a count. He chose Count Rumford for his title after the name of the New Hampshire town where he had lived.

While in Bavaria, Thompson watched workmen boring out the tube of a cannon from a cylinder of solid metal. The friction of the drilling produced an enormous amount of heat. The heat was continually produced while the drilling went on. It did not seem sensible to Thompson that heat could exist in the form of a specific quantity of fluid. Once it dissipated, where did the additional heat come from? Heat seemed to be a product of the continual motion of the grinding process. Mechanical energy was being converted into heat energy.

The specific heat of ice is .50, half that of liquid water. This means that it should take half a calorie of heat to raise the temperature of a gram of ice 1° Celsius. This works until the ice reaches the temperature of 0° Celsius and is ready to change state into water, that is, when the ice begins to melt. It takes 80 calories of heat to change one gram of ice into one gram of water, and during that process the water does not gain in temperature. At 0° Celsius, it goes from ice to water. There is a change of state but no increase in temperature, even though each gram of the ice has absorbed 80 calories of heat energy. This was called latent heat by the chemist Joseph Black. The same thing happens when water changes state from liquid water to steam vapor. To change a gram of boiling water at 100° Celsius to a gram of steam at 100° Celsius requires 540 calories of heat energy, even though the temperature of the steam is the same as the boiling water after the addition of this heat energy. In the case of converting ice to water, this 80 calories of latent heat is also known as the heat of fusion of water. In converting water to steam, this latent heat is known as the heat of vaporization of water.

At about the same time, British physicist Humphry Davy (1778–1829) performed an even simpler experiment that supported Thompson's conclusions. He placed two pieces of ice in a vacuum that had a temperature below the freezing point. Rubbing the two pieces of ice together produced friction that melted the ice despite the subfreezing temperatures. This suggested that heat could be produced by mechanical work.

Because of the widespread acceptance of the caloric theory, Thompson's and Davy's work remained largely unappreciated for a number of years. But in 1842, German doctor Julius Robert Mayer (1814–1878) wrote a paper that also suggested the equivalence of heat and mechanical work and that one could be transformed into the other. His actual experiment consisted of little more than vigorously shaking a container of water and showing that the water had a rise in temperature.

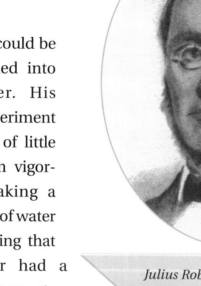

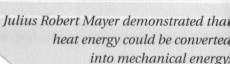
Julius Robert Mayer demonstrated that heat energy could be converted into mechanical energy.

The problem was taken up by English physicist James Prescott Joule (1818–1889) about forty years later. Joule was a fanatic at measuring the heat produced by various phenomena, and he possessed very accurate thermometers. On his honeymoon, he measured the temperature at the top and bottom of a waterfall to see if the conversion of the water's motion into heat energy at the bottom of the fall made the water there warmer.

James Prescott Joule discovered the mathematical relationship between heat energy and mechanical energy.

Joule had inherited a winery and used the wine cellars to perform heat-related experiments since the cellars had a fairly constant temperature. Joule devised an experiment in which the energy of falling weights turned paddles in water in an insulated container. The movement of the paddles imparted the energy of the falling weights to the water, resulting in a change in temperature. By 1847, he had conducted enough experiments to define what was called the mechanical equivalent of heat. Joule had determined that the temperature of one pound of water could be raised 1° Fahrenheit by 772 foot-pounds of mechanical work. In the metric system, that meant that 41,800,000 ergs of work would always produce one calorie of heat. An erg is a very small unit of energy, the amount of energy or force required to accelerate one gram of mass to a speed of one centimeter per second.

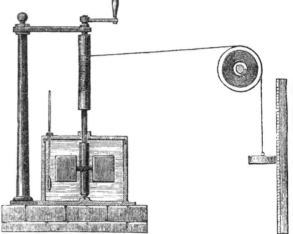

This is Joule's apparatus for adding mechanical motion to water to raise its temperature.

Experiments conducted up to this time on the motion of various machines seemed to indicate that energy disappeared as it was used. A machine might be set in motion, but if it did not receive continuous inputs of energy, it would slow down and stop. If Joule was right, however, this energy was not being lost. Mechanical

We've talked about temperature scales and how temperature is measured, but how is heat energy measured? Two units are in common usage. In the metric system, the unit of heat energy is the calorie, which is defined as the amount of heat required to raise the temperature of one gram of water 1° Celsius. This definition clearly shows the difference between heat and temperature and how the two are related. Do not confuse this definition of the calorie used by physicists with the calorie used by nutritionists. That calorie is actually a kilocalorie, equal to 1,000 of the smaller calorie units used in scientific measurement.

In the English system, the unit of heat energy is the British thermal unit, or Btu. One Btu is the amount of heat required to raise the temperature of one pound of water 1° Fahrenheit.

energy was converted by friction into heat. If heat was also a form of energy, the energy put into a machine was equal to the work done by the machine plus the heat lost in the process. Energy was conserved.

The principle of the conservation of energy was one of the most important concepts ever to be discovered by science, and it is known as the first law of thermodynamics. It states that the total energy content of a closed system remains constant. The first full statement of this principle, however, is credited not to Joule but to German physiologist Hermann Helmholtz (1821–1894), who in 1847 announced the same idea from his studies of how muscle tissue produced heat when it contracted.

THE STEAM ENGINE

By now the relationship between heat and other forms of energy was a matter of interest. One problem during the seventeenth century was the presence of water in the shafts of mines, particularly English tin and coal mines.

*Hermann Helmholtz observed that
contracting muscle tissue grew warmer.*

Thomas Savery (1650–1715) was a military engineer who became interested in trying to solve this problem. He was familiar with the work of Denis Papin (1647–1712), the physicist who invented the pressure cooker in 1679. Papin observed that steam could raise the lid of a cooking vessel, and Savery concluded that steam could perform work.

Savery designed and patented a machine consisting of a closed vessel filled with water into which pressurized steam was introduced, forcing the water to a higher level. When the water was expelled, a sprinkler condensed the steam, producing a vacuum capable of pulling more water into the vessel through a valve. In this way, water could be pumped out of mine shafts, and Savery manufactured a number of his engines primarily for that purpose. He titled a 1702 manuscript describing his engine *The Miner's Friend.*

English engineer Thomas Newcomen (1663–1729) recognized some limitations to Savery's engine, particularly its weakness under high steam pressure. He experimented for more than ten years, finally building an improved steam engine in 1712. In Newcomen's engine, steam pressure drove a piston upward. Then cold water sprayed into the cylinder condensed the steam and created a partial vacuum that allowed atmospheric pressure to push down the piston. Since Savery had received a broad patent for his invention, Newcomen could not patent his improved engine. But Savery recognized the value of Newcomen's improvements and they entered into partnership to produce better steam engines. Although the Newcomen engine was a great improvement over Savery's original steam engine, it was still only about 1 percent efficient, meaning that a lot of energy

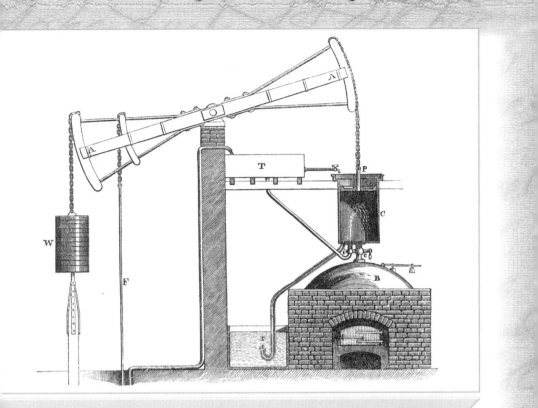

Newcomen's steam engine was designed to draw water out of mine shafts.

had to be used in order to pump water from a mine. Nonetheless, no other improvements in steam engine technology occurred for fifty years.

In 1764, Scottish inventor James Watt (1736–1819), sometimes given credit for the invention of the steam engine, was making scientific instruments at the University of Glasgow. A friend brought him a Newcomen engine for repair, and after returning it to working order

Watt observed how inefficient the machine was. Watt realized the problem with the engine was that it used the same chamber for both producing steam by boiling water and condensing the steam back to water. Since

James Watt redesigned and improve the efficiency of Newcomer steam engin

the same chamber had to be alternately heated and cooled, Watt saw that this resulted in a considerable waste of energy. In 1769, he received a patent for an improved steam engine that featured a condensing chamber separated from the boiler. Having a separate condensing chamber meant that the cylinder with the piston did not have to be reheated after each stroke. Oil lubrication of the

Young James Watt was fascinated by a pot of boiling water at his family's table.

cylinder also added to the efficiency of the Watt engine. Most important, however, Watt didn't just use his engine to create a vacuum pump to lift water from mine shafts. He discovered how to attach a rotating shaft to the piston and convert its up-and-down motion into rotary motion. This rotary motion could turn wheels and drive belts continuously.

Watts's actual steam engine (left) *and a diagram* (above).
The flywheels show how the up-and-down motion
of the piston can be converted to rotary motion.

The improved steam engines of Watt and other inventors were the main force behind the Industrial Revolution that transformed Europe from an agricultural society into an urban society and that raised living standards for many people. Steam power could drive machinery that could mass-produce goods. With the replacement of water power by steam power, factories

The father of the steam locomotive, George Stephenson (at right), *and his first steam locomotive* (above)

and mills could be built anywhere, not just near rivers. In 1814, English inventor George Stephenson (1781–1848) built the first practical steam locomotive, thus revolutionizing modes of transportation. The steam engine was proof that heat energy could be transformed into other forms of energy. It became the focus for research of many nineteenth century scientists.

Thermodynamics

One of the scientists who studied the operation of the steam engine was French physicist Nicolas Léonard Sadi Carnot (1796–1832). Looking at the steam engine from a theoretical rather than a mechanical perspective, Carnot observed a simplified picture of a machine with two heat reservoirs with different temperatures. The steam boiler had the highest temperature, and the cool water in the condensing chamber had the lowest temperature. Carnot discovered that when the steam engine was designed, the maximum possible efficiency of the engine depended on the difference in temperature between the two reservoirs. In any machine of this type, the higher the initial temperature, and the lower the final temperature, the greater the potential for an efficient conversion of heat energy into mechanical energy.

You can see that, if this is true, unless the low temperature reservoir is at a temperature of absolute zero, the efficiency of such an engine will always be less than 100 percent. Carnot published his findings in 1824 in his book *Reflections on the Motive Power of Fire*. For most of his life, Carnot accepted the caloric theory of heat, that heat was an insensible fluid, and so he never fully grasped where these discoveries were leading him.

This notion that a temperature difference was required to do work, and that heat energy had to flow from a region of higher temperature to a region of lower temperature in order to produce mechanical

William Thomson, Lord Kelvin

energy, intrigued other scientists. The phenomenon was studied by French engineer Benoit Clapeyron (1799–1864), German physicist Rudolf Clausius (1822–1888), and Scottish physicist William Thomson, also known as Baron Kelvin (1824–1907). The work of these scientists led to the second law of thermodynamics, the so-called law of entropy.

Rudolf Clausius first stated the second law of thermodynamics, the law of entropy.

This law can be stated in a number of different ways. It says that heat energy always flows from a region of higher temperature to a region of lower temperature, and never the other way around. Clausius stated in 1850, "When two systems are placed in thermal contact, the direction of energy transfer as heat is always from the system at the higher temperature to that at the lower temperature." In a closed system, that is, a system into which no new energy is added, energy must always "run down" and become unavailable for further work. All forms of energy can be converted into heat energy, but that is the end of the line.

Heat energy cannot be converted back into other forms of energy with complete efficiency. Heat energy will degrade, and the process cannot be reversed. Entropy is defined as a state of total molecular disorder, and in a closed system entropy is always increasing. A simple way of looking at this is to think of the world as one big hill with a number of boulders on top of it. Using the force of gravity, you can do useful work by rolling the boulders down the hill. But when all the boulders are at the bottom of the hill and can fall no farther, a state of entropy exists: No more work can be performed in this system, unless some outside force supplies the energy to lift the boulders back up the hill.

The second law of thermodynamics reaches far beyond the operation of steam engines. In a closed system, physical processes are irreversible. The only truly closed system, the only system to which new energy cannot be added, is the universe as a whole. If the law of entropy is correct, the entire universe is like a huge machine that will eventually run down. Eventually all the energy in the universe will be converted to heat and that heat will dissipate until it is evenly distributed throughout the cosmos. There will be no temperature difference between any two bodies anywhere, and no potential to perform work. This is called the "heat death" of the universe, and even today astronomers still debate whether this will be the ultimate fate of the universe.

The first two laws of thermodynamics, which state that energy can be neither created nor destroyed, that in a closed system energy will always become unavailable, and that no machine operating at temperatures above absolute zero can be perfectly efficient, mean that perpetual motion machines and other devices to generate limitless amounts of energy cannot be constructed.

The idea of machines that require little or no input of energy has fascinated people for hundreds of years. You may have heard about the man who claimed to have invented an automobile engine that will run forever on a gallon of water with a pinch of something added to it. You may have heard about the University of Utah scientists who claimed to have produced energy from nuclear fusion by running an electric current through a glass of cold water. Claims that such machines can be built should always be viewed with suspicion. Some devices make advances in reducing friction or may have a design that does in fact increase energy efficiency. But so far none have been shown to violate the laws of thermodynamics. Without some external input of energy, they must eventually slow down and stop.

THE KINETIC THEORY AGAIN

As Carnot, Clausius, and Kelvin were developing the theory of heat flow, two other scientists, James Clerk Maxwell (1831–1879) in Britain and Ludwig Boltzmann (1844–1906) in Austria, resumed work with gases begun by Robert Boyle and others. They began to consolidate all discoveries about heat to create a theory of matter to explain them. Previous scientists had discovered the relationship between the pressure and the temperature of a gas mixture. As the temperature of the gas increased, if its volume was held constant, the pressure the gas exerted increased. Maxwell and Boltzmann, working independently, each questioned the caloric explanation for heat and explained both temperature and pressure as the effects of billions of moving molecules.

In any given sample of gas, these molecules were in constant motion. Some moved very fast; some moved much more slowly. The heat content of the sample was the sum total of all of these molecular motions, fast plus slow. But temperature measured the average motion of these molecules, and a temperature reading was somewhere between the fastest and the slowest molecules. Pressure also measured the average motion of molecules as billions of them with different velocities collided with the measuring instrument. The combined work of Joule, Clausius, Kelvin, Maxwell, and Boltzmann convinced most scientists that heat resulted from molecular movement. Their efforts finally laid to rest the caloric theory of heat.

We call these principles the laws of thermodynamics, but what does that mean? A scientific law is a statement about nature that has proven to be true many times over, under varying circumstances, and which in fact has never been shown

James Clerk Maxwell supported th[e] kinetic theory of matter, that matter [is] made up of billions of tiny particle[s].

not to be true in all the experiments conducted. But is a scientific law something that has been shown to be true only in the past and that might be proven wrong with the very next experiment? Yes and no. Yes, because over the course of time, some scientific laws are found to be untrue. But this rarely happens and usually causes a great deal of debate among scientists when it does happen.

Ludwig Boltzmann

Scientific laws are broad statements about nature. But they are more than just statements that things have always occurred this way in the past. We call these statements about thermodynamics "laws" not only because they can be shown to be true in many situations, but because if they are not true, then we can't be certain about any other physical laws. If energy can be created from nothing or if energy can be destroyed, so that the total amount of energy in a closed system is unpredictable, how can we rely on other scientific statements about force and mass and distance and velocity? A simple problem that asks you to calculate the speed that a steam-driven locomotive of a certain weight can achieve becomes impossible to solve. Scientific laws are valid not only because they always seem to work, but because they fit neatly into a broader network of scientific principles and offer supporting explanations for those principles.

For this reason, once a scientific law is accepted by the scientific community, scientists are extremely reluctant to reject it. The failure of scientific laws that have achieved broad acceptance has occurred only three or four times in the history of science. There seems to be no serious challenge to the laws of thermodynamics on the horizon. Energy can be neither created nor destroyed. Despite the efforts of many misguided amateur scientists, you can't get something for nothing. And you cannot reverse the material processes going on in nature. Energy is used, and then it becomes unusable, and systems wind down unless more energy is added.

HEAT TRANSFER

Once scientists understood the concepts of heat and heat flow developed during the nineteenth century, they could better explain how heat is transferred from one body to another. People knew for thousands of years that heat could be transferred by direct contact. If you touch something hot, your hand will immediately feel hot—you may even get a painful burn. French mathematician Joseph Fourier (1768–1830) produced mathematical equations that described the rate of the flow of heat through solid objects and from one object to another. This kind of heat movement is called conduction. For conduction to take place, objects must be in physical contact. With the new kinetic theory of matter, scientists would explain conduction by saying that rapidly vibrating molecules in the hot object collide with the molecules in your hand and transfer some of their momentum to these molecules, which then vibrate faster.

Scientists work with very precise definitions of energy, work, and power, and the units with which these quantities are measured reveal how they are related. Energy is the ability to do work, and work is measured as the application of a force to move a mass a distance. So units of energy are going to be equivalent to units of work. For example, in the metric system, the unit of energy is called a joule. A joule equals a newton-meter. A meter is approximately three feet, and a newton is a unit of mass that would weigh about a quarter-pound on the surface of Earth. So if you move a quarter-pound object about three feet (horizontally, not upward against gravity), you have performed one newton-meter of work and have used up one joule of energy doing it. Power is a measure of how much energy or work you can do in a given unit of time. If you can expend one joule of energy every second, you are using one watt of power (named after James Watt).

Joseph Fourier mathematically described how heat is conducted from one object to another.

For many years, scientists have recognized a second mechanism by which heat can be transferred: convection. This occurs when a substance such as heated gas or liquid moves to another place, carrying its heat with it. Heated air, for example, becomes less dense and tends to flow in an upward direction, carrying heat to higher altitudes. Forced air heating systems in buildings also work this way: A fan blows heated air molecules to another place. It is not the energy of motion that is transferred, but the heated molecules themselves. In their new location, these molecules may transfer some of their heat to surrounding substances through conduction.

There is a third way that heat can be transferred, though the process was not clearly understood until the early twentieth century. At that time, scientists such as Max Planck (1858–1947) and Albert Einstein (1879–1955) began to explore the mysteries that James Clerk Maxwell had discovered about electromagnetism. It was noted that hot things can warm distant objects through empty space. The Sun was the prime example of this, providing heat to Earth through a 93-million-mile vacuum. But even when you sit in front of a campfire, your body is warmed by heat energy coming directly from the fire, not through the molecules of air that fill the space between you and the fire.

This kind of heat transfer is called radiation, and it differs from conduction and convection in that it requires no material medium. No molecules have to bounce against other molecules, and no molecules have to be moved to a new location for this type of heat transfer to occur. Whenever an electrically charged particle moves, it will give off waves of electromagnetic energy.

When molecules are excited, that is, made to vibrate faster by being heated, the negatively charged electrons in the orbits of the atoms of those molecules also begin to move. Their movement is of a very peculiar kind, and in fact there is no adequate physical description for what those electrons are doing. But because they "move," they give off electromagnetic waves. Some of that electromagnetic energy is in the form of light, which is what enables us to see objects. Any object at a temperature above absolute zero gives off electromagnetic radiation. An object at a temperature of absolute zero would be invisible. As more and more heat energy is added, electrons give off more energetic waves, which we perceive as a change in color of the heated object.

Some of the radiation given off by electrons is much less energetic than light waves. Just below the threshold of visible light we find a range of electromagnetic waves known as infrared waves. They cannot be seen, but they can be felt on your skin as heat.

Electromagnetic waves are a form of energy. Energy, remember, is the ability to do work, to push or pull a mass across a distance. Infrared waves are absorbed by the molecules exposed to them, and these molecules then start to vibrate more energetically just as if they had been jostled by other molecules in contact with them. In this way, heat energy is transported across empty space.

Time's Arrow

Scientists often refer to the second law of thermodynamics as "time's arrow." In measuring the length of a board, you can start at either end, or you can even start somewhere in the middle and add the distances to each end. Each way you will get the same answer. But time is not like that.

In order to measure how much time it takes for some-thing to happen, you must start at the beginning of the event and count the time to the end of the event. If an event has already happened, you may be able to figure out from recorded evidence how much time it took for that event to happen. But you cannot start your stop-watch at the end of a 100-meter dash competition and then use readings on the watch to measure how long it took the sprinters to run that distance. You cannot start at the end of an event and measure time backward to the beginning, because we go through time in only one direction, from the present to the future.

The second law of thermodynamics states that for a closed system, or for the universe as a whole, as time passes, energy is expended and becomes unavailable. It is not destroyed. It simply becomes distributed in such a way that it cannot be used to exert a force on an object and move it. This process is irreversible, unless more energy can be added to the system from somewhere else. For the universe as a whole, this is impossible.

Scientists believe that we know we are passing through time because the entropy, or disorder, of the universe is always increasing. In any physical process, some mechanical, chemical, electrical, or even nuclear energy is converted into heat and is lost in this process. Yet we know from Carnot's studies that this process cannot work the other way. You cannot convert heat energy back into mechanical or other forms of energy with 100 percent efficiency.

Earth is not a closed system. Our sun provides a constant input of new energy that is absorbed by Earth as heat. This heat sets in motion meteorological processes and stimulates the growth of living things. Differences in regional temperatures cause differences in atmospheric pressure, and pressure differences cause air masses to move from regions of high pressure to regions of low pressure. Thus the winds are born and heat energy is converted into mechanical energy. The difference in temperature between the Sun and Earth can be viewed in the same terms as the difference in

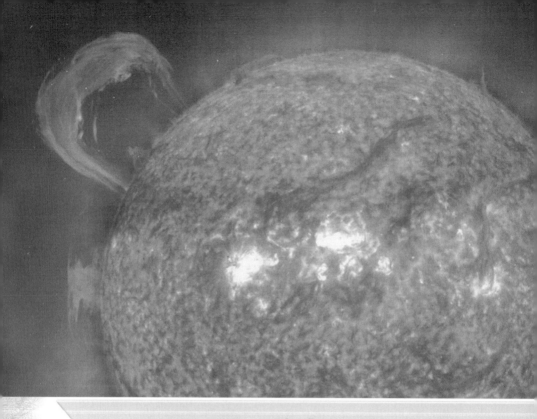

A solar flare rises from the surface of the Sun, the source of all the energy on Earth.

temperature between the boiler of a steam engine and its cooling cylinder. The heat energy of the Sun is converted into useful mechanical energy here on Earth. Much of that heat energy is first used by plants to construct their living structures. The heat energy is thus stored as chemical energy in the molecular bonds of plant tissue. When those plants die, they become layers of dead organic matter buried deep in the earth. Over time, this dead organic matter is subjected to intense pressure, turning it into coal and oil. People mine these materials and convert the chemical energy within them back into mechanical energy for use in automobiles, power plants, and so many other devices. The Sun's energy is ultimately responsible for the complex order we see in living organisms and in the artifacts of civilization. As long as the Sun shines, we have a renewable source of energy to maintain that complex order, and we can hold entropy, or disorder, at bay.

This does not mean, however, that we can ignore the second law of thermodynamics. As we use mechanical energy to do work, some of that energy is converted into heat and is lost to us forever. It ultimately radiates into space. And if, over the long term, our rate of energy use exceeds the rate at which Earth absorbs new energy, we will run out of usable energy. People will have to re-evaluate the way energy resources are used to power industrial societies. Once the energy in a barrel of oil has

This is one of the earliest automobiles with a gasoline combustion engine.

been used, that energy is gone forever in terms of its ability to do useful work. It may take millions of years to create another barrel of oil. The Sun-Earth system is, for all practical purposes, a closed system: When the Sun stops shining perhaps ten or fifteen billion years from now, no new energy transfers will sustain civilization, and life on Earth as we know it will come to an end.

The same fate may await the entire universe. It was Baron Kelvin in the late nineteenth century who first spoke of the heat death of the universe. If entropy always increases, the universe will eventually reach a state of uniform temperature and maximum entropy from which it will not be possible to extract any work. What exactly does this mean if energy cannot be destroyed? Recall our example of how the ocean holds a much greater quantity of heat energy than does a heated glass of water. The second law of thermodynamics states that heat always flows from a region of high temperature to a region of low temperature. This means that none of that heat energy in the ocean can be made to flow back into the warmer water in the glass. With respect to the glass-ocean system, the heat energy of the ocean cannot be used to perform any useful work. That energy has not disappeared. It has been evenly distributed throughout the ocean, and the average intensity of that energy, that is, its temperature, is too low to make heat flow into the glass of water. If the warmer water in the glass is poured into the ocean, the ocean will become marginally warmer, but eventually that heat energy will also be evenly distributed throughout the ocean. That is the state of entropy,

when no temperature differential exists between any two objects, and no heat energy can be made to move in order to do work. Perhaps 100 billion years from now, that will be the state of all energy in the universe.

It was Baron Kelvin who proposed that the laws of thermodynamics be the fundamental principles upon which all of physics should be based. He believed that the laws of thermodynamics expressed basic facts about the nature of energy, force, and motion that would shape all other physical processes. Today the idea of temperature is regarded as a fundamental property of matter, as fundamental a property as mass, length, and time. Furthermore, the laws of thermodynamics have led us to an evolutionary

The discovery of oil vastly increased the amount of energy available for people to use.

view of the universe. If Isaac Newton introduced the idea of a clockwork universe, Carnot, Clausius, and Kelvin demonstrated that it was a clock that was winding down and that could never be rewound. If the processes of energy transfer work only in one way and are irreversible, then time, too, is irreversible. Given a closed system and enough time, all temperature differences disappear, and no heat energy can flow. Only an outside energy source can create a new imbalance, a new temperature differential, that would cause energy to move, but there is no new energy source outside of the universe as a whole, because by definition the universe is everything.

Glossary

absolute zero The lowest conceivable temperature; the temperature at which a gas would have no volume.

barometer An instrument for measuring atmospheric pressure.

boiling point The temperature at which a liquid changes to the gaseous state.

calorie The amount of heat energy required to raise the temperature of one gram of water 1° Celsius, specifically from 14.5° to 15.5° Celsius.

energy The capacity to do work or cause heat to flow.

entropy The amount of disorder in a system.

foot pound A unit of work; the amount of work required to lift a one-pound weight one foot.

force An action that results in accelerating or deforming an object.

friction A force that opposes movement between two objects that are in contact.

gimbal A device or frame that supports an object such as a sphere or gyroscope, enabling it to spin freely.

heat The quantity of energy in a system resulting from the motion of the molecules in that system.

joule A unit of energy (or work or heat) equal to a force of one newton acting over a distance of one meter. A newton is roughly equivalent to the force exerted by Earth's gravity on a quarter-pound weight.

kinetic energy The energy possessed by an object because of its motion.

melting point The temperature at which a solid changes to a liquid.

metabolism The chemical processes by which living things grow, maintain themselves, and build new tissues.

potential energy The energy, or potential to do work, possessed by an object because of its relative position or condition.

temperature A number representing the average kinetic energy of the molecules of an object.

thermodynamics The branch of physics dealing with how heat energy moves and performs work.

thermometer An instrument for measuring temperature.

work In physics, the application of a force to move a mass through a distance.

for More Information

The three magazines listed below are sources of general science information, and often have articles about physics and thermodynamics. They can be found in the magazine section of most stores or your at local library. Each has a Web site with an "Ask the Expert" section to which you can address specific questions you may have.

Discover
114 Fifth Avenue, 15th Floor
New York, NY 10011
Web site: http://www.discover.com

Popular Science
P.O. Box 51286
Boulder, CO 80322
e-mail: askpopsci@popsci.com
Web site: http://www.popsci.com

Scientific American
415 Madison Avenue
New York, NY 10017
e-mail: info@sciam.com
Web site: http://www.sciam.com

WEB SITES

About Temperature
http://www.unidata.ucar.edu/staff/blynds/tmp.html
This site, developed for middle-school students,
explains temperature, thermometers, heat, and
kinetic theory.

Applied Thermodynamics

http://www.taftan.com/thermodynamics

This site has pages of definitions of dozens of terms related to thermodynamics, heat, and steam engines.

Classical, Quantum, Nanoscale, and Statistical Mechanics and Thermodynamics

http://tigger.uic.edu/~mansoori/TRL_html

This site is a gateway to many other sites with information about thermodynamics.

Encyclopedia of Thermodynamics

http://therion.minpet.unibas.ch/minpet/groups/
        thermodict

This is a Swiss site in English with lecture notes and tutorials related to thermodynamics.

Entropy and the Second Law of Thermodynamics

http://www.2ndlaw.com

This site discusses thermodynamics in a conversational, question-and-answer format designed to develop a sound understanding of the concept.

FOR MORE INFORMATION

First and Second Laws of Thermodynamics
http://science.clayton.edu/pratte/jmp7.html
This site has many experiments and activities that can be performed in the high-school physics classroom or lab.

The Second Law of Thermodynamics
http://www.panspermia.org/seconlaw.htm
This site discusses the relation of thermodynamics to living things.

Steam Engine Library
http://www.history.rochester.edu/steam
This is an extensive site about the history of the steam engine and includes online texts of Hero of Alexandria's *Pneumatics* and Robert Thurston's *A History of the Growth of the Steam Engine.*

for further Reading

Asimov, Isaac. *Understanding Physics: Motion, Heat, and Sound.* New York: Penguin Books, 1969.

Middleton, W. E. *A History of the Thermometer and Its Use in Meteorology.* Baltimore: Johns Hopkins Press, 1966.

Purrington, Robert D. *Physics in the Nineteenth Century.* New Brunswick, NJ: Rutgers University Press, 1997.

Sharlin, Harold. *Lord Kelvin, the Dynamic Victorian.* University Park, PA: Pennsylvania State University Press, 1979.

Sprackling, Michael. *Thermal Physics.* New York: Springer-Verlag, 1991.

Index

Credits

ABOUT THE AUTHOR

Jeff B. Moran has a Ph.D. from the University of Arkansas and has taught and conducted research in physiology, anatomy, and biochemistry. He has developed K–12 curriculum materials in all areas of science and is the composer of numerous songs about a wide range of scientific topics.

PHOTO CREDITS

Cover © Menau Kulyk/Science Photo Library; cover inset © Scott Smith/Index Stock Imagery; p. 9 © Tom Mareschal/The Image Bank; pp. 19, 48, 54, 55, 56, 59, 61, 62, 63, 65, 67, 81 © Northwind Picture Archives; pp. 35, 44, 70, 71, 77 © Bettmann/Corbis; pp. 64, 66, © Hulton-Deutsch Collection/Corbis; p. 76 © Archive

CREDITS

Photos; p. 88 © SOHO-EIT Consortium, ESA, NASA; p. 90 © Corbis; p. 92 © Ewing Galloway/Index Stock Imagery. Diagrams on pp. 8, 25, 39 by Geri Giordano.

DESIGN AND LAYOUT

Evelyn Horovicz

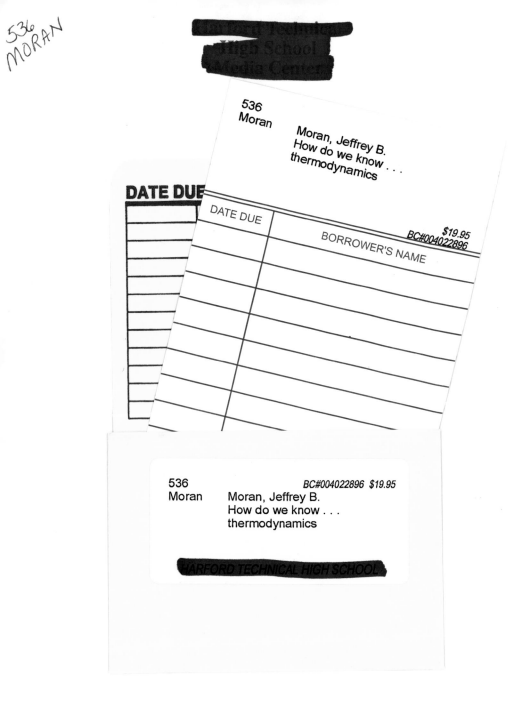

536
MORAN

Harford Technical High School Media Center

536
Moran

Moran, Jeffrey B.
How do we know . . .
thermodynamics

$19.95
BC#004022896

DATE DUE

DATE DUE	BORROWER'S NAME

536
Moran

BC#004022896 $19.95
Moran, Jeffrey B.
How do we know . . .
thermodynamics

HARFORD TECHNICAL HIGH SCHOOL